THE PHILOSOPHY OF
CHOCOLATE

THE PHILOSOPHY OF
CHOCOLATE

SAM BILTON

First published 2023 by

The British Library

96 Euston Road

London NW1 2DB

Text copyright © Sam Bilton 2023

Illustrations copyright © British Library Board 2023

and other named copyright holders

ISBN 978 0 7123 5434 9

eISBN 978 0 7123 6846 9

Cataloguing in Publication Data

A catalogue record for this book is available

from the British Library

Designed and typeset by Sandra Friesen

Printed in the Czech Republic by Finidr

CONTENTS

INTRODUCTION

Chocoholic (noun): a person who loves chocolate and eats a lot of it.

Cambridge Dictionary

MANY PEOPLE LIKE chocolate. Some even profess to love it to the point of addiction. Whether you are a lover or a hater (yes, they do exist) it is hard to imagine a world without the brown stuff.

In many respects, the fact that chocolate is part of our lives at all is something of a miracle. Early encounters with cacao were far from auspicious. In 1503 Spanish bibliographer Ferdinand Columbus, second son of the famous Genoese explorer, Christopher (1451–1506), described cacao beans as 'almonds', which, he observed, the native Maya valued as a form of currency, as did the Aztecs. Back then an avocado was worth between one and three beans, depending on its ripeness, and a turkey hen would set you back 100 beans. Neither he nor his father appreciated the true worth or the uses of cacao in the New World, effectively dismissing the beans as irrelevant before moving on to other pastures in search of gold. Columbus senior died in 1506 having never tasted the drink that just over a century later would take Europe by storm. According to English Dominican friar Thomas Gage (c.1600–1656), his fellow countrymen had an even more contemptuous attitude to cacao. On seizing a shipment of cacao from the Spanish in 1579, they ditched the cargo overboard, believing it to be worthless sheep dung.

The 'almonds' or 'dung' in question were cacao seeds or beans. When cacao pods are fresh the intensely bitter seeds are coated in a sweet, juicy pulp. The fleshy seeds are left to ferment for a number of days, which allows the pulp to liquify. The remaining seeds are dried, then roasted, becoming darker and less astringent. Finally, the outer shell of the seed is removed in a process known as winnowing. The resultant nibs are ground to create what we recognise as the beginnings of chocolate. These four stages of cacao production have remained the same for thousands of years, although much of the processing is now mechanised.

As the sixteenth century progressed and more Spaniards arrived in Central America, the invaders came to understand that the 'almonds' were also used to create a drink favoured by the Mayan and Aztec elite, a taste they had gained themselves from the Olmecs (1500–400 BCE). Unsweetened, murky and brown this

cacahuatl was an acquired taste. The word cacahuatl comes from Nahuatl, a native language of central Mexico, and means 'cacao water'. In his *History of the New World* (1575), Girolamo Benzoni (*c.*1519–1572), a Milanese merchant and adventurer, described chocolate as 'more a drink for pigs, than a drink for humanity'. However, in the absence of wine, the Spanish gradually became accustomed to drinking it, adding Old World spices like cinnamon, pepper and anise with plenty of sugar to compensate for the natural bitterness cacao possesses.

Even once the Spanish had adopted and augmented this beverage, cacao proved a tricky product to farm. Cacao is an exceedingly fussy plant: it will only bear fruit within a narrow band from 20 degrees north to 20 degrees south of

the equator, which is why it thrives in Central America and parts of Africa and Asia. It cannot tolerate any altitude that causes the temperature to fall below 16°C, or that is too dry, plus it is susceptible to disease and pests. Even the Aztecs had to import cacao, as the central highlands of Mexico lacked the optimum climate to grow these trees. All in all it is something of a surprise that chocolate has achieved the prominence it has in our lives today.

There are several words used to describe chocolate at various stages of its production. Swedish naturalist Carl Linnaeus (1707–1778) classified the tree on which the curious pods grow as *Theobroma cacao*, meaning 'food of the gods' in Greek. In this book *cacao* refers to the raw, unrefined state of the beans from the pods. Once the beans have been processed and pulverised to extract most of the fat, known as cocoa butter, they become *cocoa*, such as the powder you would use as an ingredient in a chocolate cake. Liquid or solid preparations of cocoa are defined here as *chocolate*.

So how did chocolate captivate our hearts? Is it simply a matter of taste or is there a more emotional attachment? In the following pages we will journey through some of the reasons why chocolate has enthralled us for centuries. It is a tale of spirituality, conviviality and seduction – at times with sinister undertones. Empires have been founded and destroyed in its name.

Chocolate has a long, complex and fascinating history, which certainly merits further exploration. To this end there is a suggested, but certainly not exhaustive, reading list at the close of this book to help you on your onward path of discovery.

SPIRITUAL CHOCOLATE

It took four men ... to conduct the happy chocolate to Monseigneur's lips. One lacquey carried the chocolate-pot into the sacred presence; a second, milled and frothed the chocolate with the little instrument he bore for that function; a third, presented the favoured napkin; a fourth (he of the two gold watches), poured the chocolate out. It was impossible for Monseigneur to dispense with one of these attendants on the chocolate and hold his high place under the admiring Heavens.

Charles Dickens, *A Tale of Two Cities* (1859)

THE MAYANS BEGAN using cacao somewhere between 600 and 400 BCE, although it was probably an integral part of Mesoamerican belief systems from a much earlier date. In the *Popol Vuh* ('Book of Counsel'), an ancient manuscript that records the mythology of the K'iche' Maya, cacao is listed as one of the ingredients used by the great 'Begetter' to create human flesh. Offerings of cacao were made to the god of sustenance, K'awiil. It was also used in a form of baptism witnessed by the Franciscan bishop Diego de Landa (1524–1579), where Mayan children had their heads, faces, fingers and toes anointed with water infused with flowers and cacao. So, in many ways, Linnaeus' classification of the cacao tree was very apt.

The Aztecs, who flourished between 1325 and 1519 CE, also used it in ceremonies and as a tribute to gods like Tlaloc, the god of rain, thunder and lightning. Spanish Dominican friar Diego Durán (1537–1588) provided a gruesome account of a feast held by merchants of Cholula in Mexico to honour the feathered serpent god Quetzalcoatl, the symbol of death and resurrection. A handsome slave was selected to represent Quetzalcoatl on earth for forty days. As befitting a god's ambassador, the slave was suitably pampered, receiving beautiful clothing, jewels and sumptuous food and drink. His only job was to dance and sing his way through the streets each day, receiving adulation from the crowds as he went. Naturally, there was a catch to this short taste of the Aztec high life. At the end of his tenure as Quetzalcoatl, the slave would be forfeiting his life (he was locked up at night in case he got any ideas about escaping). He was expected to accept this news with equanimity and continue his daily gambol in a joyous manner. Should he show any signs of wavering in his commitment, the slave would be given a special chocolate drink made with blood-stained water previously utilised to clean the obsidian knives used in human sacrifices.

Whatever the drink contained, it caused the slave to forget about his impending doom and resume his cheerful demeanour until the fateful day. Following the sacrifice, an offering of the slave's heart was made to Quetzalcoatl, and his flesh was cooked and served at the chieftain's banquet.

Stories like this were probably retold (and the more macabre elements possibly exaggerated) by the likes of

Durán to illustrate just how much the indigenous people of the New World needed Christianity. Although the religious offensive to convert the 'heathens' sought to wipe out their gods and festivals, vestiges of Aztec celebrations can still be found today. Durán was disheartened to note that the Aztec festivities surrounding Miccailhuitontli (Little Feast of the Dead, which honoured innocent but unbaptised children) and Miccailhuitl (Great Feast of the Dead, for the deceased adults) had been transferred to All Saints (1 November) and All Souls (2 November) respectively. On these days the native population made offerings of flowers, food and chocolate to honour departed family members. 'I suspect that if it is an evil simulation ... the feast has been passed to the Feast of Allhallows in order to cover up an ancient ceremony,' he wrote. The Día de los Muertos festival is still celebrated with great pomp in Mexico today, and the *ofrenda* (offering) includes bread, cakes and sugar figures. Chocolate features too as a drink, and as moulded chocolate skulls and commercial chocolate bars. It is also a classic ingredient in *mole*, a rich turkey stew made with chillies, tomatoes and spices, often served during the celebratory meals.

The conquistadors did a pretty thorough job of annihilating the indigenous people of Mesoamerica. Nevertheless, there are some tribes today who still follow a lifestyle that has changed little over the centuries, such as the Kuna of the Panamanian San Blas islands. The customs of the Kuna were observed by anthropologist Professor

James Howe over a forty-year period, beginning in the 1970s. This tribe ritualistically burns cacao to communicate with the spirit world. A seer, or *nele*, uses the smoke to look into this other-worldly dimension to divine the cause of an illness or problem. When a member of the community is ill, the Kuna believe their soul has been kidnapped by evil spirits. A shaman who has learned 'the Way of Cacao' burns some beans and chants to invoke the female cacao-spirit. The spirit battles with the evil presence and rescues the soul, returning it to the patient's body. To the Kuna, cacao is as crucial today in their defence against malign beings as it was four hundred years ago.

The chocolate consumed by the Mayans and Aztecs was very different to our idea of drinking chocolate today. The cacao nibs were ground to a paste using a grinding stone called a metate, along with flowers (such as the ear-shaped petals of the *Cymbopetalum penduliflorum*), vanilla, achiote (a natural orange-red food colourant) and chillies. The paste was first infused in hot or cold water. The mixture was then strained and poured between two vessels to create a head. The foamy chocolate was drunk out of brightly coloured calabash cups, generally by the higher echelons of society. Sugar was unknown to these civilisations prior to the arrival of the Spanish, so the unsweetened drink was very bitter. The Spanish persevered and eventually embraced chocolate, putting their own sugar and spice spin on the native drink. The nuns of Oaxaca were talked of 'far and near' for their skill in making chocolate: so great was their renown that their lozenges of chocolate were shipped to other parts of Mexico and even back to Spain.

The Spanish soon realised that this exotic drink could satisfy hunger as well as slake thirst, particularly when mixed with maize. Consequently, the nourishing nature of chocolate would vex the Roman Catholic Church for centuries. If by drinking chocolate a person could go without any other sustenance for long periods, should it be considered a food? If it were a food, then surely it was not appropriate to drink chocolate during fasting periods such as Lent? This was particularly the case for religious orders who followed a very limited and bland diet during this time. The conundrum provoked much debate in the sixteenth century, with Pope Gregory XIII (head of the Roman Catholic Church from 1572 to 1585) and several of his successors decreeing that drinking chocolate did not break the fast so it remained an acceptable beverage during Lent.

Not all religious communities agreed with this stance or indeed the general consumption of chocolate. Superior General Mutio Vitelleschi (1563–1645), head of the Society of Jesus, or Jesuits, from 1615 until his death, spent decades trying to enforce a ban on chocolate within his order, particularly for those ministering in Mexico. The objections to chocolate included its extravagance, which flouted the order's rules of poverty, and its association with women, who were chiefly responsible for preparing

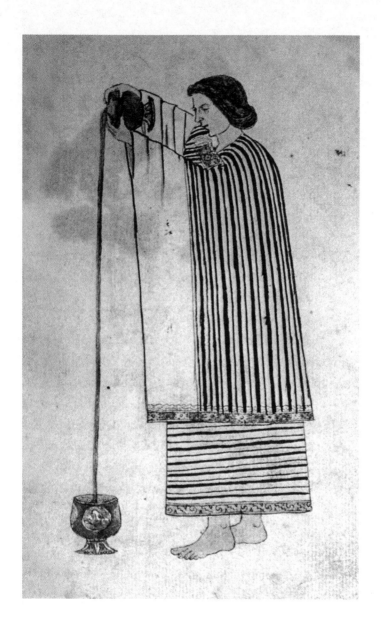

it, and links to witchcraft. Jesuits were ordered to eschew chocolate in all circumstances, even illness, despite it being respected by European physicians as something of a super-food at this time. Vitelleschi wrote countless letters berating the Jesuit provincial representatives in Mexico for allowing the chocolate abuse to continue on their watch. But to no avail. Even the threat of expulsion from the order did not curb the use of chocolate among the Jesuits, which continued into the following centuries. Father Julio Ortiz of the Jesuit College in Mexico City requested 50 pounds of chocolate from his superiors for Easter 1688. Chocolate was clearly much in demand.

Perhaps Vitelleschi's concerns were well founded. Bishop Bernardino de Salazar y Frías (d.1626) found to his cost just how beloved chocolate was to the wealthy ladies of Chiapas. The ladies claimed that they were unable to get through an entire mass without a cup of chocolate to sustain them, which their servants would duly deliver mid service. This incensed the bishop, who threatened to excommunicate the women if they did not desist from the practice. Several of the ladies ignored the bishop's threats and, as Thomas Gage puts it, continued 'drinking in iniquity in the church, as the fish doth water'. This resulted in an altercation where swords were drawn when priests attempted to forcibly remove the cups of chocolate from the ladies. Not long after this incident Bishop Salazar became ill and died in excruciating pain. It was later revealed that he had been given a cup of poisoned chocolate by a servant who was in cahoots with one of the gentlewomen. The incident gave rise to the proverb 'beware the chocolate of Chiapas'.

The dark colour and grainy texture of chocolate made it an ideal vehicle for delivering poison and spells. In Guatemala between the sixteenth and eighteenth centuries there are several accounts of witchcraft perpetrated by women involving chocolate. In most cases the aim was to secure the devotion of a particular man. In 1705 Francisca and Juana de Agreda, a wealthy mother and daughter, were accused by one of their servants of making an ensorcelled chocolate drink for Francisca's lover, the parish priest. The drink was said to contain hair, fingernails, saliva and pubic hair. Almost 250 years later a 'witch' was used to advertise chocolate by Rowntree's, albeit an attractive blonde with bedroom eyes proffering two cups of cocoa to her spellbound husband. It ran with the tagline 'My Wife's a Witch!' – something you certainly would not have exclaimed in Francisca's day (unless you wanted shot of your wife, of course). Colombian novelist Gabriel García Márquez (1927–2014) captures the mystical power this drink could convey in his book *One Hundred Years of Solitude* (1967), when Father Nicanor levitates after downing a cup of thick, steaming chocolate. The trick raises enough money from the locals in one month to begin the construction of a church.

As chocolate infiltrated the courts of Catholic Europe, it became associated with this more ostentatious form of Christianity. Who would think that the peace-loving, plain-speaking, protestant Quakers would become chocolate entrepreneurs? In terms of earning money, going into business was the logical option for Quakers in the eighteenth and nineteenth centuries. As non-conformists they were not permitted to attend Oxford or Cambridge universities, or become Members of Parliament. Nor could they join the armed forces, as they were pacifists. Some Quaker families like Cadbury and Rowntree created chocolate empires that are still in existence today (albeit now subsumed into larger confectionery conglomerates). Their success sat at odds with Quaker principles, which advocated wealth creation should be for the benefit of the workers, local community and society at large rather than for individual gain alone. Both Joseph

Rowntree (1836–1925) and George Cadbury (1839–1922) campaigned against poverty and social injustice. They took a paternalistic approach to their workforces to redress the balance, building garden cities like Bournville, just outside the city of Birmingham, where the workers lived and socialised. Neither organisation was beyond reproach and both would be touched by scandal in the twentieth century.

It may not have supernatural powers but there was definitely *something* about chocolate that made some people hot under the collar.

LE BAIN.

De la Lettre ou du Chocolat   J'ai le cœur bien plus délicat
Que préfère Madame? Ah ma chere Justine,   Plus foible infiniment, hélas! que la poitrine.

A Paris chez Buldet rue de Genres.

SEDUCTIVE CHOCOLATE

Chocolate goes very well with sex: before, during, after
– it doesn't matter.

Helen Gurley Brown, editor of
Cosmopolitan (1986)

WHAT IS IT ABOUT a food that makes it sexy? The greyish-white amorphous oyster with its snot-like texture and salty tang rouses little in me beyond disgust. And yet, this mollusc has been touted as one of life's great aphrodisiacs for centuries. Based on appearances alone, solid brown chunks of chocolate do not promise a great deal in terms of sexiness. Place a square of good, dark chocolate on your tongue and feel it slowly dissolve into silkiness as the cocoa butter melts, allowing the enchanting aromas to pervade your senses. This is when chocolate begins to get sexy, and you can understand why it has been hyped as an aphrodisiac. 'There is nothing as aphrodisiac as a mousse au chocolate on the skin,' according to Chilean writer Isabel Allende in *Aphrodite: A Memoir of the Senses* (1998).

When conquistador Bernal Díaz del Castillo (1492–1584) wrote *The True History of the Conquest of New Spain* (1568) he helped create chocolate's reputation as an aphrodisiac. He related a story of the Aztec king Moctezuma II (*c*.1466–1520) drinking chocolate before visiting his many mistresses and two wives to fortify him for the rigours ahead. Aphrodisiacs stimulate sexual desire, which leads to copulation and ultimately, it was hoped, conception. In ancient times at least they were more about boosting fertility than producing pleasure. Chocolate featured at important Mayan feasts and ceremonies, like weddings. A folktale from the Alta Verapaz region of Guatemala has foamy chocolate being exchanged by a married couple to seal their marriage vows. This has echoes of a scene depicted in the Madrid Codex – one of three surviving pre-Columbian Maya books – of Chaak (the rain god) marrying Ixik (the earth goddess). Even today a K'iche' bridegroom is expected to bring a gift of cacao to the wedding feast held at his in-laws' house. After Aztec wedding ceremonies the bride and groom were led to their bedchamber and four days of feasting followed, during which chocolate drinks were served. The Aztecs prepared chocolate in several different ways but only one, *atextli* – a herbal chocolate drink, was thought to have aphrodisiac properties, although the active agent may well have been one of the herbs rather than the cacao itself.

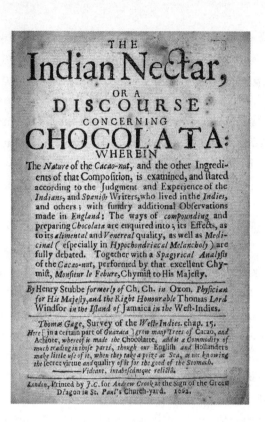

THE
Indian Nectar,
OR A
DISCOURSE
CONCERNING
CHOCOLATA:
WHEREIN

The *Nature* of the *Cacao-nut*, and the other Ingredients of that Composition, is examined, and stated according to the Judgment and Experience of the *Indians*, and *Spanish* Writers, who lived in the *Indies*, and others; with sundry additional Observations made in *England*: The ways of *compounding* and preparing *Chocolata* are enquired into; its Effects, as to its *alimental* and *Venereal* quality, as well as *Medicinal* (especially in *Hypochondriacal Melancholy*) are fully debated. Together with a *Spagyrical Analysis* of the *Cacao-nut*, performed by that excellent Chymist, *Monsieur le Febure*, Chymist to His Majesty.

By Henry Stubbe *formerly of* Ch. Ch. *in* Oxon, *Physician for His Majesty, and the Right Honourable* Thomas L*or*d Windsor *in the Island of* Jamaica *in the* West-Indies.

Thomas Gage, Survey of the *West-Indies*. chap. 15.
Here [in a certain part of *Guaxaca*] *grow many Trees of Cacao, and* Achiote, *whereof is made the* Chocolatte; *and is a Commodity of much trading in those parts, though our* English *and* Hollanders *make little use of it, when they take a prize at Sea, as not knowing the secret virtue and quality of it for the good of the Stomach.*
——*Videant, intabescántque relíctâ.*

London, Printed by *J.C.* for *Andrew Crook* at the Sign of the Green Dragon in St. *Paul's* Church-yard, 1662.

Francisco Hernández (1514–1587) was adamant that chocolate excited the venereal appetite. This posed a potential problem for religious orders, like the Jesuits, who favoured abstinence from sex, hence Vitelleschi's campaign against it. However, much of the clergy and Europe's elite were happy to turn a blind eye to chocolate's saucy credentials. In some cases, its lusty qualities were seen as a positive boon.

In *The Indian Nectar* (1662) English royal physician Henry Stubbe (1632–1676) contradicted the views of others in his profession who saw chocolate as an aphrodisiac. Chocolate on its own, he concluded, did not provoke lust. As a plain drink it provided health benefits for men and women. It was more effective than bleeding a patient or giving them medicine, especially in cases of depression. The drink only became lustful when 'hot' spices were added, such as cinnamon, pepper and chilli. Stubbe grumbled that some purveyors of chocolate added so many spices to the preparation that they 'reduce chocolata almost to Ginger-bread'. His preferred way of taking chocolate was to mix it with water, sugar and perhaps an egg. When he was feeling particularly adventurous, he would throw in a splash of orange flower water or sherry. He did concede that mild 'Jamaican spices', like vanilla, were beneficial additions to the drink.

Stubbe was confident enough of chocolate's innocuous properties to suggest it was suitable for women, most definitely considered the weaker sex in his day, particularly those suffering from hysteria or love melancholy. When Madame de Pompadour (1721–1764), mistress to Louis xv (1710–1774), feared the virile French king was losing interest in her she took up a diet of celery soup, truffles and chocolate. 'Sometimes he thinks I am like a *macreuse*' (a waterfowl, said to have cold blood), she confided to her friends. She hoped the diet would warm up her temperament and increase her libido. Throughout her life

Some of the more renowned licentious associations with chocolate in the eighteenth century are connected to two continental gentlemen. The Italian lothario Giacomo Casanova (1725–1798) drank chocolate most mornings before he set off on his various conquests, but perhaps even more notorious is the Marquis de Sade (1740–1814). One tale has him feeding some guests at a ball with chocolate pastilles laced with *cantharides* (Spanish fly, which is actually a type of beetle). The story goes that the evening quickly descended into a frenzied orgy; however, the truth was less erotic. When crushed and applied externally, *cantharides* is believed to create sexual arousal but also causes irritation and even blistering. When ingested, it can lead to vomiting and internal bleeding and was used in the past to procure abortions. In some cases it can be fatal. The Marquis' guests were prostitutes who became violently ill after eating the pastilles and reported him to the authorities. De Sade fled to Italy, and although the poisoning charges were dropped, he was sentenced to death in absentia and burned in effigy. He returned to France in 1777 when his mother died, was promptly arrested and spent the rest of his days in prison. De Sade had a sweet tooth and a particular penchant for chocolate: 'I asked … for a cake with icing,' he wrote to his wife 'but I want it to be chocolate and black inside from chocolate as the devil's ass is black from smoke. And the icing to be the same.'

Madame de Pompadour was plagued by chest infections and suffered three miscarriages during her liaison with the king. Despite the fact their sexual relationship ended in 1750, the two remained close friends until she died at the age of 42 from tuberculosis.

So is there any truth in the aphrodisiac claims?

Cacao contains theobromine, an alkaloid closely related to caffeine, considered to be a mood enhancer and energy booster. But the chemical that really turns people on is phenylethylamine (PEA), or the 'love drug'. This is thought to be present in high concentrations in the brains of people who are happy or in love. It has been suggested that this is why those disappointed in love seek solace in chocolate. Phenylethylamine is another alkaloid that influences the 'happy hormones' such as dopamine and serotonin in the brain. It stimulates the hypothalamus, inducing pleasurable sensations, thus enhancing your sex drive. 'Chocolate's sensual, hedonistic connotations undoubtedly make it a suitable companion for sex. Simply believing in its aphrodisiac powers should be enough to get the juices flowing, regardless of any real pharmacological effects,' concludes Paul Martin, author of *Sex, Drugs and Chocolate* (2014). However, he and most of the scientific community seem to agree that, as yet, chocolate's aphrodisiac powers have not been conclusively proven.

HEALTHY CHOCOLATE

Psst ... Chocolate is Good.

Evening Standard, 13 April 2012

THIS IS THE SORT of headline that has chocolate lovers rejoicing. When chocolate receives an 'official' stamp of approval from scientists, we can toss away our guilt and health concerns about eating it like a crumpled wrapper.

One of the most renowned studies on the health benefits of chocolate was conducted by Dr Norman Hollenberg (1936–2020), a medical professor for Brigham and Women's Hospital and Harvard Medical School. He observed that Kuna tribespeople from remote islands off the Panamanian coast had lower blood pressure and therefore lived longer than their compatriots who had migrated to cities on the mainland. The key dietary difference between the two groups, observed Hollenberg, was the amount of chocolate they consumed.

With funding from Mars, Inc., Hollenberg studied the Kuna's dietary habits during the 1990s. He discovered that individual island Kuna were drinking at least five cups of chocolate per day, and it was the primary beverage consumed by the islanders. The chocolate drink was made from cacao grown on the islands, which was rich in flavonoids, particularly epicatechin. Flavonoids occur naturally in plant pigments that are common in fruit, tea, red wine and cacao beans. They are powerful antioxidants, which can help protect your body against cardiovascular diseases, like hypertension, as well as diabetes.

Much less chocolate was consumed by the mainland Kuna. They drank commercial chocolate products purchased in stores rather than from home-grown cacao. The processing methods used to create these products reduces the concentration of the flavonoids. Therefore, the mainland Kuna were not benefitting from drinking chocolate to the same degree as their island cousins. These Kuna were more likely to have high blood pressure, particularly as they aged. Dr Hollenberg was convinced that the consumption of flavanol-rich chocolate was largely responsible for the differing health standards between the island and mainland Kuna.

Hollenberg was not the first scientist to deduce the healthiness of chocolate. For the Aztecs cacao served as a medicine as well as a beverage. It was used to treat intestinal complaints, fever, faintness and coughs, to name but a few.

By the mid sixteenth century chocolate had found its way to Europe. Francisco Hernández, physician to Phillip II of Spain, decreed cacao had cool and humid properties. Working on the principle that you could balance out adverse symptoms of an illness or environment with ingredients possessing opposing qualities, chocolate was considered an excellent drink for hot weather and for those suffering from a fever. It was mostly prepared with other flavourings, like vanilla, cinnamon, chillies or pepper, and the majority of these were deemed to be hot. This nicely balanced out the cool nature of cacao, although occasionally their effects went too far in the opposite direction, provoking lustful urges.

The Spanish had conquered their initial aversion to the bitter, muddy liquid by adding sweeteners. A spoonful of sugar really did help the medicine go down. However, they began to realise that sweetened chocolate drinks tasted good – *really good*. So much so that it became a pleasurable and, in time, incredibly fashionable beverage among the elite classes across Europe. The fact that chocolate could confer health benefits too was simply the cherry on the top.

From Spain, the habit of drinking chocolate spread to courts across Europe. Marie Gigault de Bellefonds, Marquise de Villars, was the wife of the French ambassador at the Spanish court of Charles II (1661–1700). In her letters back to France Madame de Villars described chocolate as her only pleasure in this foreign land. She followed a careful chocolate diet even during Lent, prompting her to declare that 'le chocolat est une chose merveilleuse' (chocolate is a wonderful thing). Britain's Charles II (1630–1685) is said to have paid £200 (thousands of pounds today) in the mid seventeenth century for a particular chocolate recipe. As a devout Catholic, the suitability of chocolate as Lenten fare vexed France's Louis XIV (1638–1715). He eventually acquiesced and welcomed chocolate at court, perhaps influenced by his queen and his brother Philippe, Duc d'Orléans, who loved the stuff, although the king himself preferred herbal infusions. In Italy, the secretive physician Francesco Redi created jasmine-scented chocolate for Cosimo III de' Medici (1642–1723), Grand Duke of Tuscany, which Redi kept under lock and key until his death.

One of the reasons for chocolate's success was the nourishment it provided. This was largely down to the fat content of cacao. The downside was that the fat was insoluble and could leave a greasy layer on the surface of the drink. To emulsify the cocoa butter with the liquid, starches such as maize or wheat flour could be added. This made the drink even more substantial, although later generations would question whether the addition of starch constituted adulteration. Chocolate was considered beneficial for invalids, particularly where weight gain after illness was desirable, and to aid digestion or strengthen weak stomachs. In *The Natural History of Chocolate* (1725), originally published in French and translated by physician Richard Brookes, there is a story of a women from Martinique who had lost her lower jaw and was unable to eat solids. She positively thrived on three 'dishes' of chocolate a day flavoured

with cinnamon and sugar and was livelier and more robust than she had been before the accident. Chocolate could also provide a remedy to the ageing process. According to another account in the book, a Martiniquais lived to one hundred after consuming nothing but chocolate, biscuit and a little soup (no fish, flesh or other food) for thirty years. He remained nimble and vigorous and at the age of 85 was still able to get on horseback without stirrups.

William Hughes, a seventeenth-century horticultural writer and privateer (essentially a pirate with royal approval to pillage other nations' vessels), wrote a study on the fauna of the Caribbean, particularly Jamaica, that included an extensive account of the cacao tree and on how to make chocolate. In *The American Physitian* (1672) he described chocolate as the 'most Excellent Nectar'. He observed that sailors who arrived in the Indies after a long voyage in poor physical health made a remarkable recovery after drinking chocolate. All levels of society drank the beverage, including 'the meanest servants', before going to work to ensure they could last out until their dinner at 11am. Hughes asserted that it was possible to subsist on chocolate alone providing it was drunk at least twice a day. Chocolate was an excellent drink for people with weak constitutions, such as those suffering with consumption, and was especially suited to hot climates thanks to its refreshing nature.

However, while Hughes was thoroughly convinced of the merits of chocolate in tropical climates, he was less

enthusiastic about its use in his homeland: 'I not think it so convenient to be too frequently drunk here in England by those who are in health and full strength because our hotter stomachs require not food of so easie a digestion, being naturally strong enough to dispence with that which is more solid.' But if chocolate was merely a wholesome food, what mischief could come of drinking it?

Henry Stubbe had also encountered chocolate while serving as His Majesty's Physician in Jamaica and echoed Hughes' concerns about the drink. Stubbe thought that if a person followed a sensible diet, and took regular exercise, chocolate taken in moderation would do no harm. However, if it were drunk for wantonness rather than necessity, chocolate could make an individual unwell. In such cases, the patient would become pale, giddy, tremble and suffer from headaches. While he conceded that adding warm spices to the cold-natured cacao was essential to help with the digestion of chocolate, he felt some were more beneficial than others. Achiote, the red colourant used by the Aztecs, was good for strengthening the stomach, but chilli pepper could inflame the blood and was particularly hazardous for young folks.

On 15 April 1671, the Marquise de Sévigné, Marie de Rabutin-Chantal (1626–1696), wrote to her daughter to warn her of the ills of chocolate:

> I want to tell you, my dear child, that chocolate is no longer with me as it was: fashion has carried me away, as it always does: all those who spoke well of it to me speak ill of it; we curse it, we accuse it of all the evils we have; it is the source of vapours and palpitations; it flatters you for a time, and then suddenly kindles you with a continuous fever, which leads you to death.

Whatever health concerns were raised about chocolate, they did little to dampen the public's enthusiasm for the product. In the nineteenth century chocolate was still marketed as a healthy beverage. At one stage Cadbury's tried adding Irish moss to their cocoa essence. A type of seaweed, Irish moss is thought to improve the immune system; however, consumers seemed less than convinced by the claims and eventually the product was dropped. Chocolate was used to mask the tastes of other medicines well into the twentieth century, featuring in restorative lozenges for consumptives, iron supplements that included tiny pieces of metal, vermifuges like Dawson's Chocolate Creams, or laxatives which can still be purchased today.

So, the question remains, is chocolate good for you? Although Hollenberg's study of the Kuna points to chocolate having a positive effect on human health, other scientists are more reticent to espouse its virtues until further evidence has been gathered. James Howe argues that similar results relating to low blood pressure have been found in studies of other indigenous populations who do not consume chocolate. His view is that the Kuna islanders have lower blood pressure because of their active lifestyle and low-fat, fish-based diet, rather than eating one particular foodstuff. The study of chocolate and its impact on human health is complex and, at times, contentious. The overarching view appears to be that eating small amounts of dark chocolate on a regular basis will do no harm. This is not quite the same as saying chocolate is good for you, but it is as much of an endorsement as you are likely to get from the modern scientific community at present.

HOSPITABLE CHOCOLATE

Every whiffler in a laced coat, who frequents the chocolate-house shall talk of the constitution with as much plausibility as this very solemn writer.

Jonathan Swift, *The Publick Spirit of the Whigs* (1714)

ON WEDNESDAY 24 April 1661, the diarist Samuel Pepys (1633–1703) awoke with the hangover from hell. The day before had been spent drinking, eating and drinking some more to celebrate the coronation of Charles II. 'Waked in the morning with my head in a sad taking through the last night's drink, which I am very sorry for,' he lamented in his diary. Fortunately, his friend John Creed was on hand to give him some chocolate to settle his stomach. Indeed, chocolate would continue to serve as a remedy for those who had 'drunk too deeply of the cup of pleasure' well into the nineteenth century, as gastronome Jean Anthelme Brillat-Savarin (1755–1826) put it.

Pepys appears to have developed a liking for this new drink, possibly after receiving an anonymous gift of 'a quantity of chocolate' in June 1660. Initially, he drank it in the morning at his own lodgings or a friend's. However, on 24 November 1664 he records drinking 'jocolatte, very good' at a coffee house. The first coffee house in London had been established by Pasqua Roseé, a Greek servant to a Levant Company merchant named Daniel Edwards, in 1652. They were places for men of business to gather to read about and discuss the latest news over a dish of one of the 'new' exotic, non-alcoholic drinks that included chocolate and, on occasion, alcohol. Towards the end of the seventeenth century, dedicated chocolate houses like Ozinda's and White's would join the array of coffee houses in London and other British cities.

In theory anyone with the means to pay for the drink was welcome at these establishments, helping these beverages move out of aristocratic circles and into the broader social melee of the middling sorts. By choosing to visit a particular chocolate house you were effectively nailing your political colours to the mast. The Cocoa Tree and Ozinda's Chocolate House were considered Tory haunts. White's Chocolate House was a Whig hangout. Some people, like James Brydges, the first Duke of Chandos (1673–1744), were more concerned about the quality of the clientele than their political affiliations. He was known to attend Ozinda's and White's as well as several other coffee

and chocolate houses in the fashionable area of St James's in London. If there was no one worth talking to when he arrived, he would simply move on to the next establishment in a kind of Enlightenment café crawl.

By the early eighteenth century chocolate houses had taken on a decidedly decadent character aimed more at pleasure seekers than business doers. According to *The Tatler* on 12 April 1709, 'All Accounts of Gallantry, Pleasure and Entertainment' were to be found at White's. Those who were more interested in foreign and domestic news, learning or poetry should decamp to a coffee house. White's gained a reputation for cards and gambling. Plate VI of Hogarth's *A Rake's Progress* (1732–1734) shows

Tom Rakewell, a miscreant, squandering the last of his inheritance at the gaming tables in White's as the neighbouring houses in St James's burn. The rest of the gamblers are so engrossed in their game, they are oblivious to the smoke filling the room despite the frantic efforts of the night watchmen. The original location of White's did indeed burn down in 1733. The manager's wife, Mrs Arthur, leapt out of a second-floor window onto a feather bed to escape the flames. Thankfully, she was unharmed.

Chocolate house customers became the butt of satirical jibes in the papers and pamphlets of the day. They were portrayed as effeminate fops or beaus, flamboyantly clothed, doused in powder and obsequiously polite. They were often depicted as French men, taking their lead from the decadent court of Versailles. In *An Essay in Defence of the Female Sex* (1696) the fop flounces into a chocolate house 'scented like a perfumers shop'. He proceeds to spend fifteen minutes gazing at himself in a mirror, before snorting some snuff with an exaggerated flourish. His conversation is frivolous – of fashion or gossiping about other lords and ladies he had recently encountered at balls. The 'masculine' men of England, free from the vices of wealthy foreigners, possibly preferred coffee (despite the fact it was thought to cause impotence), although the documentary evidence left by likes of Pepys and Brydges suggests otherwise.

Chocolate houses like White's gradually became private members' clubs. To gain admittance you had to be

proposed by an existing subscriber, voted in by the existing members and pay an annual subscription fee. By 1775 this was ten guineas, ensuring only the wealthiest society men could become members. White's is still in existence today as an exclusive gentleman's club, although its days of serving drinking chocolate are long gone.

The move from voguish social hangout to selective club could have spelled the end of the chocolate house, but they would re-emerge in the next century, albeit in a more sober guise. The temperance movement gained traction in the nineteenth century, as non-conformist religious groups, such as the Methodists, and prominent Quaker chocolate makers, like John Cadbury and Joseph Rowntree, railed against the drunkenness which they believed had become the scourge of society. 'Public houses play a larger part in the lives of the people than clubs or friendly societies,' bemoaned social reformer Charles Booth (1840–1916). In the absence of an alternative, pubs provided the perfect venue for labouring men and women to socialise over a beer at the end of a day's work.

Chocolate was seen as the perfect non-alcoholic antidote to disorderly behaviour. Technological advances

and reduction in duties would see cocoa becoming more affordable, with British consumption increasing sixfold between 1870 and 1910. Although much of this was drunk at home, cocoa rooms and coffee palaces began to spring up around the country, providing an alternative to the pub. The reformed chocolate houses were spacious and had a touch of Continental style about their décor, with marble counters, large mirrors and chandeliers. When a second Lockhart's Cocoa Room opened in Sunderland in August 1878 it boasted a bar area serving non-intoxicating drinks, a smoking room and lavatories. Liverpudlian metal broker turned philanthropist Robert Lockhart (c.1821–1880) had already opened nine cocoa rooms in Newcastle, Sunderland and South Shields in the space of the year, as well as those in his home town. He was delighted to inform the assembled guests at the Sunderland launch that in one week alone they had served 35,000 cups of tea, coffee or cocoa. Since opening the cocoa rooms, staff had received 702 teetotal pledges, where customers had agreed to give up alcohol entirely. 'There was nothing like keeping temptation as far away as they could,' he quipped.

Charitable-minded people could purchase tickets or tokens for the cocoa rooms as a form of donation for less fortunate individuals. This allowed the poor who could not afford to buy the food and drink themselves to procure a cup of cocoa and something to eat. It was hoped this system of charity, operated by organisations like the

Ladies Temperance Prayer Union, would prevent the need for soup kitchens. Even away from the refreshment rooms chocolate was frequently doled out to impoverished children. At the Watercress and Flower Girls' Christian Mission established near Covent Garden by John Groom in 1866, the girls received a free mug of cocoa before they started work early in the morning. Wesleyan missions also offered cups of cocoa to encourage children forced to work to attend evening classes to make up for the education they were missing.

For a fleeting moment it appeared the offensive against the public house by the cocoa rooms and coffee palaces would oust them from society. But the pub began to fight back, offering their customers non-alcoholic drinks alongside beer as well as hot and cold food. The previously squeaky-clean reputation of the cocoa rooms was occasionally tarnished by allegations of gambling, resulting in a £5 fine for a Liverpool cocoa room manager, Harry Clement, in 1922. In 1920 the manager of Lockhart's Cocoa Room in Peckham was bludgeoned with a hammer in a botched burglary. Whether it was incidents like these or a general shift away from temperance, the popularity of alcohol-free 'refreshment' houses waned in the twentieth century and the attraction of the pub never truly disappeared.

FEMININE CHOCOLATE

Twill make Old women Young and Fresh;
Create New-Motions of the Flesh,
And cause them long for you know what,
If they but Tast of Chocolate.

James Wadsworth, in *Chocolate: or,*
An Indian Drink (1652)

THROUGHOUT HISTORY women have been depicted as being obsessed by chocolate. In his introduction to the translation of Antonio Colmenero de Ledesma's *Curioso Tratado de la Naturaleza y Calidad del Chocolate* (1631), writer and bungling spy James Wadsworth (b.1604) boldly stated that chocolate was adored by the female sex. Besides helping the drinker put on weight (this was an era when being plump was seen as a sign of health), it made her good-humoured, lustful, fertile and could even ease labour. Henry Stubbe claimed to have encountered numerous cases in nunneries where women suffering from hysteria, melancholy or fatigue had been treated with chocolate. He was also an advocate of vanilla, a spice added to chocolate, which eased the symptoms of menstruation and enhanced intelligence.

Around the same time as Wadsworth and Stubbe were extolling the virtues of this beverage, references to chocolate start appearing in household manuals and manuscripts. These were either aimed directly at, or written by, women who were the guardians of the household's health and well-being. These documents contained culinary and medicinal recipes, such as one belonging to Rebeckah Winche dated 1666. Rebeckah was married to Sir Humphrey Winche, 1st Baronet (1622–1703), Member of Parliament for Bedford. She provides an early recipe for chocolate (or 'chacolet' as she calls it) which includes cinnamon, chilli, sugar, vanilla, musk and ambergris, providing precise measurements for each, which is unusual for recipes of this time. In the popular recipe book *The Queene-Like Closet* (1672), Hannah Woolley (1622–*c*.1675) mixes her 'Chaculato' with claret wine, egg yolks and sugar.

Although women were not officially excluded from chocolate houses, they were more likely to drink chocolate at home. Chocolate was the drink of the boudoir, especially in the morning. Venetian painter Pietro Longhi (1701–1785) captured such a scene in *La cioccolata del mattino* (Morning Chocolate). It features a young woman reclining in bed with her lap dog and two gentlemen in attendance about to be served a cup of chocolate. In English poet Matthew Prior's (1664–1721) 'Hans Carvel', the young

THE
QUEENE-LIKE CLOSET
Or
RICH   CABINET

Printed for Rich: Lownes
at the White Lion in Duck Layne neare West smithfield 1670.

45

wife of the 'impotent and old' Hans was 'wak'd at ten; drank chocolate, then slept again'. French ladies of the leisured class in the eighteenth century wouldn't dream of taking their morning draught of chocolate before eleven. Brillat-Savarin believed that chocolate aided digestion, particularly after breakfast, allowing ladies to dine in comfort a few hours later, adding: 'Persons who drink of chocolate regularly are conspicuous for unfailing health and immunity from the host of minor ailments which mar the enjoyment of life.'

In 1995 dietitian and nutrition expert Debra Waterhouse released *Why Women Need Chocolate*. She explains that women have always had special nutritional needs that lead them to crave particular foods, but above all chocolate. When serotonin and endorphin levels are low, women can feel irritable, moody, stressed and fatigued. Foods high in sugar and fat, like chocolate, can boost these 'brain' chemicals. Chocolate is also emotionally linked to reward (especially in childhood), solace (when hurt or unwell) and affection (such as giving or receiving it as a gift). Waterhouse says it is a combination of psychological and biological factors that drives our love affair with chocolate.

Early assertions by the likes of Stubbe that chocolate can help with menstruation may not have been unfounded. Some women do report craving chocolate immediately prior to and during the first day or two of their periods. Hormone fluctuations during the transition to menopause

MORNING or the REFLECTION.

The magic charms of Night are past,
The sweet delusion flies,
Next Mermaids......... thoughts arise
Satan...... Horrible .....

can also intensify these cravings. Both circumstances are characterised by low levels of progesterone and oestrogen.

The sexually stimulating nature of chocolate, particularly in regard to women, was observed by Wadsworth and his contemporaries, but some modern writers maintain there are women out there who would choose chocolate over sex. 'Whereas women used to be obsessed about sex, they now are preoccupied with thoughts and fantasies about food,' claim Rosalyn Meadow and Lillie Weiss in *Women's Conflicts About Eating and*

Sexuality (1992). 'The desire to eat and the desire for sex share that compulsive driven quality, the body moving as though of its own will.'

This intense desire for chocolate has been likened to addiction. Although chocolate contains mild psychoactive ingredients like theobromine, the quantities are so minor that you would need to eat nauseating amounts to experience any effects, positive or otherwise. Like many species humans are predisposed to hanker after sweet fatty foods, such as milk chocolate. Milk chocolate serves as a form of sugary self-medication, which is why some people seek comfort by eating it when they are down. It is the sweetness rather than the cacao that drives the craving. Ultimately, giving into this desire to eat chocolate can leave some feeling guilty and more depressed than they were beforehand.

By the second half of the nineteenth century, women's attraction to chocolate was being noted by chocolate manufacturers. Cadbury's were the first of the major Quaker chocolate firms to use advertising to promote their products. Fry's and Rowntree's were uncomfortable using these exploitative methods to generate sales, believing the quality of their products spoke for themselves. Using the tagline 'ABSOLUTELY PURE—therefore BEST', Cadbury's advertisements featured images like winsome, plump-cheeked children enjoying a cup of their cocoa. The aim was to pull at a women's heartstrings – how could a mother possibly deny her child such a nutritious drink?

THE BEST BEVERAGE FOR CHILDREN

CADBURY'S COCOA is closely allied to milk in the large proportion of flesh-forming and strength-sustaining elements that it contains. It is prepared on the principle of excluding the superabundance of fatty indigestible matter with which Cocoa abounds—supplying a refined thin infusion of absolutely pure cocoa, exhilarating and refreshing, for Breakfast, Luncheon, Tea, or Supper—giving staying power, and imparting new life and vigour to growing Children, and those of delicate constitutions. "A perfect Food."—Health.

CADBURY'S COCOA
ABSOLUTELY PURE—therefore BEST.

The idea of the conscientious housewife and mother still featured in some twentieth-century advertisements, but others were aimed at young women who worked or enjoyed active leisure pursuits. In 1937 a Cadbury's advert suggested that female typists should eat a bar of Dairy Milk for their elevenses to remain pert and alert for the rest of the day. Those who declined would be lacklustre and less productive than their chocolate-fuelled counterparts. It was suggested that the additional milk made these energy-boosting bars extra nutritious. Rowntree's had their own nourishing bar in the form of the Chocolate Crisp (better known as KitKat). KitKat advertisements from the 1930s displayed women enjoying activities like golf or cycling. With the strapline 'The Biggest Little Meal in Britain!', KitKat promised two hours of steady nourishment for 2d.

As the century progressed the importance placed on the nutritive aspects of chocolate declined. Chocolate was increasingly marketed as an indulgence, whether it was to treat a child (Cadbury's 'a finger of fudge is just enough to give your kids a treat') or a reward ('a Mars a day helps you work, rest and play'). Women were never far from the narrative, though. Some of the most famous television adverts for Cadbury's confectionery were for their Flake chocolate bar. As early as 1959, they featured a beautiful woman seductively eating the 'crumbliest, flakiest' chocolate (which, let's face it, in the real world means shedding messy chocolatey crumbs everywhere after the first fateful bite that tend to melt in all the wrong places). A gratuitous close-up of the model's glossy lips as she takes a lingering bite from the bar was a given. The implicit sexual undertones of these advertisements have caused more than a few raised eyebrows over the decades; Cadbury finally withdrew the famous strapline and 'Flake girl' concept in 2010. Women continue to be a key target market for chocolate confectionery, but especially boxed assortments sprinkled with a sugary dusting of romanticism.

ROMANTIC CHOCOLATE

'Have a bonbon?' He took out of his pocket a pretty
little inlaid box, and placed it open on the table.
'Chocolate a la Vanille,' cried the impenetrable man,
cheerfully rattling the sweetmeats in the box, and
bowing all round.

Wilkie Collins, *The Woman in White* (1859)

WHENEVER YOU GET close to finishing a box of assorted
chocolates there are usually one or two flavours lingering.
In my house it is always the strawberry- or orange-flavoured
fondants. (Why do chocolate makers persist in producing
these varieties?) Like the last kid to be picked for team
sports at school, these stragglers have been consistently
overlooked in favour of the more enticing caramels, fudges
and truffles.

The Quaker Fry brothers from Bristol were chocolate
innovators. In 1847 they had created the first solid chocolate
bar. Their biggest coup came when they launched their
chocolate-covered minty cream sticks in 1853. Shopkeepers

FRY'S MILK CHOCOLATE.
"Unrivalled as a Chocolate Confection."- *Medical Magazine*.

Fry's PURE CONCENTRATED *Cocoa*

The Original First.   Established 1728.
"THE MOST PERFECT FORM OF COCOA."- *Guy's Hospital Gazette*.
MAKERS TO HIS MAJESTY THE KING, HER MAJESTY THE QUEEN, H.R.H. THE PRINCE OF WALES, TO SEVERAL ROYAL COURTS OF EUROPE, AND TO THE PEOPLE FOR NEARLY 200 YEARS.

and consumers had never seen anything quite like it before. The segmented rich dark chocolate bar filled with a smooth fondant centre soon became a popular confection. Twenty years later Fry's were credited with producing the first hollow chocolate egg in Britain. In 1923 the Fry's name would be attached to the original fondant-filled Creme Egg (marzipan and marshmallow fillings were available too), although technically they were made by Cadbury's with whom Fry's had merged in 1918.

Fry's competitors were not resting on their laurels while the Bristol firm churned out new products. Recognising the popularity of chocolates with creamy fillings, George (1839–1922) and Richard Cadbury (1835–1899) launched their Fancy Box of chocolate fondants in 1868. The chocolates had French-sounding names like Chocolat des Délices aux Fruits and were packaged in a silk-lined velvet box, topped with a suitably mawkish image featuring cute creatures or cherubic children. Whereas Fry's Cream Sticks could be picked up at a local confectioner for a few

I n *The Rituals of Dinner* (1991) Margaret Visser describes how an ephemeral box of chocolates is an ideal gift to provide a dinner host. 'A durable and inappropriately valuable gift would upset the delicate imbalance created by a dinner invitation,' she explains. The quandary posed to the host is whether they should share that gift with the guests or save it for themselves to enjoy later and run the risk of looking greedy. The attitude to this dilemma varies across the world. North Americans are sharers, Visser observes, whereas in Turkey a hostess wouldn't dream of diverting her attention away from her guests by opening a gift.

pennies, the Cadbury's Fancy Box was designed to exude class and luxury with a suitably extravagant price tag. It was the perfect gift for a special person; a custom that continues to this day.

As well as being a token of appreciation, giving a box of chocolates could be interpreted as a romantic gesture. For much of the twentieth century it formed part of the courtship ritual between a man and a woman portrayed in advertisements. Men gave their significant others a box of chocolates to show how much they cared, or to apologise for some minor misdemeanour. Chocolate firms like Rowntree's catered for all budgets and aspirations: Dairy Box, containing an assortment of milk chocolates, was the budget option aimed squarely at the working-class man who could spend a shilling to keep his 'Sweetie' sweet; Rowntree's Black Magic was a more aspirational product – with its stylish black box it was marketed as the assortment favoured by the society ladies but at an affordable price. In perhaps the ultimate act of chocolate chivalry, Cadbury had a chisel-jawed man in black performing death-defying feats to deliver chocolates to his amour, 'And all because the lady loves Milk Tray.'

The Japanese take a slightly different approach to giving chocolates. On Valentine's Day it is women who bestow gifts of chocolates, but not just to their lovers. Since the 1950s there has been a tradition for female workers to give their male colleagues *giri choco* ('obligation chocolates')

Two heads with but a single box

BUT WHAT A BOX!—A daintily ribboned box of Barker & Dobson Verona
Chocolates—the Chocolates blended by
experts for your gratification, containing
centres of Fruits. Almonds, Fruit Creams,
Pralines, Liqueurs, etc., all blending most
delightfully with the delicious, smooth
Verona chocolate.

She is pleased with them and with his
choice of what he knows she likes best.

BARKER & DOBSON LTD., Makers since 1834, LIVERPOOL

*In attractive
ribboned boxes*

*Barker
Dobson*

1 lb. box 5/- 2 lb. box 10/-
Also 3 lb. and 4 lb. boxes.

VERONA
CHOCOLATES

A word of explanation:

Black Magic are the special new Chocolates which over 3,000 chocolate-lovers judged "best" — even against 5/- a pound assortments. By using this simple sophisticated black box, instead of fancy expensive decorations and tinfoil, Messrs. Rowntree's are able to sell Black Magic at 2/10 a pound, 1/5 a half, or 9d. a quarter.

to express their appreciation for their co-workers' help and support. As it would be unfair (some would even say unwise) to single out one man for this honour, many women often end up giving multiple gifts, potentially making this a tiresome and expensive custom. In recent years there has been a bit of a backlash against this practice. In 2018 Belgian chocolatier Godiva took out a full-page advertisement in the Japanese press, stating 'Valentine's Day is supposed to be a day when you tell someone your pure feelings. It's not a day on which you're supposed to do something extra for the sake of smooth relations at work.' In the 1970s 'White Day', celebrated annually on 14 March, was launched. This gives male workers an opportunity to reciprocate the gesture by buying their female colleagues white cakes or sweets such as marshmallows, although some women prefer scarves, handbags or pearls. In 2019 a survey found that only 31 per cent of Japanese women would be giving *giri choco*, choosing to give *honmei choco* – true feelings chocolates – to their partners instead. Perhaps Godiva's efforts to reignite the romance of Valentine's Day were not in vain after all.

An anonymous gift of chocolates is suggestive of a secret admirer, but some attentions are less welcome than others. While starring in a play at London's Savoy Theatre in 1920, vaudeville actress Peggy O'Neil (1898–1960) received an unbranded box of chocolates. As there was no note with the gift, she assumed they had been sent by a friend. 'They looked particularly fresh and tempting [so]

I ate two or three,' she told police later. She even gave her little dog, Blue Boy, one as a treat. During the performance she experienced dizziness and stomach cramps and was rushed to hospital, although the doctors were confused as to what was ailing her. When Blue Boy was discovered by Miss O'Neil's maid, dead in a corner of her dressing room, poison was suspected. It transpired the chocolates had been laced with arsenic and strychnine and that Miss O'Neil was fortunate not to have shared the same fate as her dog. Her would-be assassin was never identified. 'I shall never open another parcel,' vowed Miss O'Neil. 'It has given me a terrible fright, because I did not know I had an enemy in the world, let alone London.'

So, yes, chocolates can spell romance, but as Forrest Gump's mother astutely observed, you never quite know what you're going to get.

POISONOUS CHOCOLATE

*The poisoned chocolate in an anonymous packet is a
familiar criminal device.*

Weekly Dispatch (London),
Sunday 12 November 1922

PEGGY O'NEIL WAS not the first, nor the last, person to fall
foul of doctored sweets. In the early 1920s there was a spate
of chocolate-related poisonings. Attempts were made on
the lives of the Chief Commissioner for the Metropolitan
Police, a vice-chancellor at Oxford University and a
solicitor in Hay-on-Wye, all through the medium of toxic
fondant-filled chocolates.

Unsurprisingly the poisoned-chocolate plot device
frequently crops up in fiction. In *The Count of Monte
Cristo* (1845) by Alexandre Dumas (1802–1870), Gérard
de Villefort, the ambitious public prosecutor responsible
for sentencing Edmond Dantès to life in prison, fears his
villainous wife is trying to poison him when she sends him
an unexpected cup of chocolate. Although this particular

cup is untainted it later emerges that his suspicions were not unfounded. Agatha Christie's Belgian detective, Hercule Poirot, struggles to unravel 'The Clue of the Chocolate Box' published in *The Sketch* in 1923, featuring – you guessed it – poisoned chocolates. The case occurs during Poirot's early years in the Brussels police force and is the only one he failed to solve. John Dixon Carr's (1906–1977) *The Black Spectacles* (1939) was inspired by a real-life chocolate poisoning in Victorian Brighton, which we will return to later.

Before the likes of Fry's had launched their chocolate cream sticks, the poison vehicle of choice was liquid chocolate. Industrial innovations of the nineteenth century would improve the texture of chocolate, but in earlier eras it could be gritty and bitter. In short, it was the perfect disguise for poison, and as a result it was often the primary suspect in a questionable death. When Louis XIV's grandson Charles, Duc de Berry (1686–1714) died after vomiting black blood, rumours circulated around Versailles that he had been poisoned by chocolate. The duke had been hurt the previous day in a hunting accident but had not consulted a physician. The following morning, he drank copious amounts of chocolate before going out hunting as usual. It appears he had sustained serious internal injuries from the earlier accident and died shortly after returning home. In another unsubstantiated tale, Jesuits were accused of poisoning Pope Clement XIV's

hot chocolate in 1774. The pope, who was terrified of assassination, had been instrumental in suppressing the Jesuit order in 1773. It was suggested the poisoning was a reprisal for this act. However, the autopsy failed to prove the claims.

Hell hath no fury like a woman scorned, and many ladies have shown just how effective chocolate can be as a tool for revenge. Marie-Catherine Le Jumel de Barneville (c.1650–1705), Countess d'Aulnoy and renowned spinner of fairy tales, illustrated this perfectly in one gruesome story of a passionate Spanish lady spurned in love. On cornering her former lover, she was gracious enough to let him choose between a dagger or poisoned chocolate as his mode of demise. He chose the latter, although suggested she add more sugar to mask the bitterness the next time she used poisoned chocolate. The lady stood by while the man died in agony, just to make sure the poison had done its job properly.

In 1857 Glaswegian socialite Madeleine Smith was mortified to discover that her much older ex-boyfriend, Pierre Emile L'Angelier, planned to expose their sexual relationship to her family. So much so, she allegedly slipped a lethal dose of arsenic into his cocoa. Although there was extensive correspondence between the two revealing the scope of their intimacy, there was scant evidence to suggest the two were together on the night or even the days before L'Angelier died. Madeleine was acquitted and became something of a celebrity after the trial, receiving regular requests for her autograph and ten marriage proposals. Stage actor H. B. Irving (1870–1919) claimed to have met Madeleine when she was an elderly lady in the early twentieth century. He told his friend, writer Somerset Maugham (1874–1965), that Madeleine had confessed to murdering L'Angelier and said she would happily do it again if she needed to.

Perhaps the most notorious chocolate poisoner is Christiana Edmunds (1828–1907). Christiana was what some people today would call a stalker. Outwardly, she

VIEW OF THE HOUSE AND MADELEINE SMITH HANDING A CUP OF CHOCOLATE
FROM HER BED-ROOM WINDOW TO L'ANGELIER

appeared to be a respectable, middle-class spinster who lived with her widowed mother in Brighton, East Sussex. Inwardly, simmered a scheming, malicious soul who would stop at nothing to achieve her aims. Around 1869, she befriended Dr Charles Beard and his wife Emily. Christiana soon became obsessed with the family doctor, writing him long love letters. Dr Beard declared later that it was a one-sided love 'affair', but for Christiana the only obstacle between her and happiness was his wife. Emily had to go.

In September 1870 Christiana decided to make a social call to Emily, bearing a gift of chocolate creams. She was most insistent that Emily eat the chocolates while she was there. Fortunately, the chocolate had a foul, metallic taste and Emily spat it out. She became ill later, and her husband suspected that Christiana had attempted to poison his wife with arsenic. When confronted by the doctor, Christiana denied the claims, stating that the fault must lie with the shopkeeper, Mr Maynard. Dr Beard now realised just how toxic Christiana's affections were and forbade her to have any further contact with him or his wife.

Now fearful that she would lose her beloved doctor forever, Christiana set out to repair her relationship with Dr Beard. All she had to do was prove that Emily's poisoning was not an isolated case. Using messenger boys, Christiana ordered more chocolate creams from Mr Maynard. She injected them with strychnine then asked the boys to return them to the shop on the pretext that she had ordered the wrong ones. As the chocolates appeared to be in perfectly good order Maynard put them back on display. Some of these chocolates were bought by Charles Miller, who gave them to his four-year-old nephew, Sidney Barker. Shortly after eating the chocolate creams, Sidney suffered torturous convulsions. Twenty minutes later he was dead. Christiana testified at the inquest into the boy's death that she had also experienced ill-effects from eating chocolates bought from Mr Maynard. As the shopkeeper did not make the chocolate himself the coroner concluded that the contamination had occurred during manufacturing at the supplier's factory (strychnine was used to kill vermin in workshops). Maynard was ordered to destroy his stock of chocolate creams but was otherwise cleared of any wrongdoing. Sidney's death was effectively ruled as an accident.

The verdict did not convince Dr Beard, who still flatly refused to have anything to do with Christiana. His rejection propelled her to take further poisonous action. She sent packages of tainted sweets, cakes and even fresh fruit to people in Brighton, such as Mr Garrett, the chemist she had bought the poison from, and even to herself. Several people became seriously ill, although there were no further fatalities. With a serial poisoner on the loose, the Brighton constabulary offered a reward for information. The messenger boys and chemist came forward and Christiana was linked to the crimes through the handwritten notes she had sent to the latter.

In January 1872 Christiana Edmunds was found guilty of the murder of Sidney Barker. Although the recipients of her poisonous parcels had been adults, she was portrayed in the media as a predatory child killer. Her crime was described as the 'most diabolical act' ever conceived. Initially, she was sentenced to death but this was later commuted to life imprisonment in Broadmoor Asylum on the grounds of insanity. She lived out her remaining days in this institution relatively quietly except for the odd complaint about not having access to make-up or her own clothes (her doctors often described her as being vain). She never showed any remorse for her crimes.

Chocolate may have been an ideal vehicle with which to convey poison but it was not always easy to prove that it was responsible. Wealthy widow Elizabeth Downing died in November 1816 from suspected poisoning at the hands of her son-in-law, Robert Donnall. A surgeon by trade, Donnall, who was deep in debt, had informed his creditors that he would soon come into money as his mother-in-law was seriously ill. In fact, Elizabeth was in good health and did not fall ill until consuming a cup of cocoa at her daughter Harriet Donnall's house. Mr Donnall was accused of somehow poisoning her cocoa with arsenic. He had been very cagey after the woman's death and tried to prevent a post-mortem by having her buried quickly. His explanation for his behaviour was that he feared Mrs Downing had died from the highly contagious disease cholera. Donnall somehow managed to wheedle his way into the post-mortem, which was conducted by another surgeon. This provided him with the opportunity to tamper with the evidence, meaning no trace of arsenic could be found. Although Mrs Downing had displayed all the classic symptoms of poisoning, without any proof the case against Donnall was circumstantial at best, so the jury found him not guilty.

Deadly poisons and human detritus aside, all manner of things could find their way into chocolate, and while they may not have been adverse to health, they were cause for concern.

FRAUDULENT CHOCOLATE

*To such perfection of ingenuity has this system of
adulterating food arrived, that spurious articles of
various kinds are everywhere to be found, made so
skilfully as to baffle the discrimination of the most
experienced judges.*

Friedrich Accum, *A Treatise on the Adulterations
of Food and Culinary Poisons* (1820)

WHEN POET JOHN DRYDEN (1631–1700) arrived in London
in 1658, he was keen to immerse himself in city culture.
Chocolate, he had heard during his days at Cambridge,
was the 'thing' that all the fashionable, intellectual types
were drinking these days. He headed to the nearest coffee
house where he understood this new-fangled drink could
be procured. The landlady was accustomed to serving
young whelps in her establishment, so wet behind the ears
it was as if they had just been birthed. Never missing an
opportunity to profit from their *naïveté* she gave Dryden
a dish of coffee instead of chocolate, charging him the full

three pence, which was twice the price of the former. If the lad were cannier than he looked and discovered her ruse, she would claim it was an honest mistake. The drink was all Dryden had heard it would be – dark, bitter and slightly gritty. As far as he was concerned, he was drinking chocolate, and so the deception continued for two years.

In Dryden's day tea, coffee and chocolate were new and rare commodities. Aside from the treatises written by the likes of Stubbe and Wadsworth, people relied on word-of-mouth descriptions. Pepys had been fortunate enough to have been introduced to chocolate by his friend John Creed, but for many their first encounter with these drinks was in a coffee or chocolate house. Whether the drink served was genuine coffee, tea or chocolate is anyone's guess.

It was hardly surprising that vendors of these new exotic beverages found ways to make them go further to increase their profit. It has been suggested that one of the reasons the English made their chocolate with milk and eggs rather than water as the Spanish did was to extend the product. Peanuts were roasted and ground with a little cocoa in Spain to create a cheap version of chocolate for the poor. Roasted peanuts have a similar flavour profile to cacao, which is why the Spanish call them *cacahuete*. In the southern states of America a similar recipe was used during the Civil War (1861–1865) when cacao to make chocolate was unavailable. Tea, coffee and chocolate were heavily taxed, making them expensive. In 1728 the

household accounts for Cannons in Edgware, the estate of James Brydges, reveal that £1 13s was spent on 6 pounds of chocolate, but the duty totalled a whopping £4 16s. Chocolate was also a rarer commodity than coffee or tea and was imported in much lower quantities, ensuring that it remained expensive and ultimately open to abuse.

One of the first to comment on the sullying of chocolate was the French pharmacist Antoine-Augustin Parmentier (1737–1813). In 1803 Parmentier published an essay in which he noted the qualities of inferior chocolate. Good chocolate should melt in the mouth and 'leave a kind of freshness'. It should not feel gritty or pasty on the tongue, nor should it congeal when cool. If it did, it signified that the cacao had been mixed with some sort of starchy matter. If the chocolate was excessively bitter, it indicated that the beans were under-ripe or over-roasted. Exposure to sea water could also damage the beans and adversely affect their flavour. A cheesy scent revealed the presence of animal fats like tallow, commonly used to make candles, and could turn the chocolate rancid. Analytical chemist John Mitchell continued the campaign to eradicate food adulteration in his *Treatise on the Falsifications of Food* (1848). With regard to chocolate, he notes that while most adulterants were harmless in themselves, they interfered with the nourishment available from the drink. However, some adulterants, like red lead used to enhance the colour of the drink, were highly injurious to health. Mitchell provides a number of tests that can be performed to detect adulterants. For example, if a small sample of chocolate mixed with a weak acetic acid like vinegar effervesced, then chalk, used as a bulking agent, was present.

The question of what exactly constituted an adulterant was a thorny issue for many chocolate manufacturers. The hazardous items like red lead were obvious no-nos but what about harmless sugar and starch? A report from the Lancet Sanitary Commission published in 1855 found that only eight of the fifty-six samples analysed were what they considered genuine cocoa. Over 80 per cent contained some form of starch and sugar, including those from renowned firms like Fry's and Cadbury's. Starch, be it from potatoes, sago, wheat or arrowroot, was added (argued the manufacturers) to prevent the fat separating in the liquid and make the product easier to digest. The commission rejected this claim. In their opinion the addition of starch and sugar was simply a means of bulking out the product to increase profit. However, neither the starch nor the sugar were technically damaging to health. They also objected to any mixture of cacao, starch and sugar being referred to as cocoa, stating it was 'manifestly … improper and deceptive'. They suggested the English manufacturers follow the example of the French, who referred to such preparations as chocolate, reserving the word cocoa for the raw material.

Unsurprisingly, chocolate manufacturers were keen to stress the purity of their products. Forward-thinking organisations like Cadbury took out advertisements expounding the quality of their cocoa. One that appeared in the *Birmingham Daily Gazette* on 19 March 1867 stated that Cadbury's Cocoa Essence was 'genuinely pure' and 'free from … the numerous adulterations used to counterfeit it'. Fellow chocolate makers Dunn & Hewett went a step further and offered to pay a forfeiture of £50 to a charity if their 'Unadulterated Chocolates' were found to contain anything other than cacao, sugar and starch. They continued to vehemently protest against the ruling that starch should be labelled as an adulterant, maintaining that it was essential to make the product digestible.

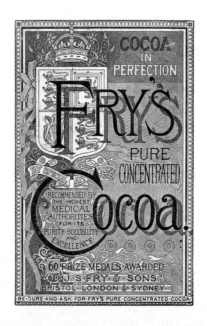

Dunn & Hewett were particularly concerned that grocers rather than the wholesalers were being brought to task over selling compound cocoas as a result of the Food Adulteration Act (1872), which they felt did little to address the 'real and abominable adulterations often practised'.

One practice Dunn & Hewett were particularly concerned about was the inclusion of cacao seed husks in cocoa. The outer husks of the cacao beans were usually discarded after roasting and crushing, leaving the nibs for processing into cocoa. Charles Hewett claimed the fibrous husks could irritate the stomach and lead to vomiting, so had no place in genuine cocoa. However,

CADBURY'S COCOA
"The typical Cocoa of English manufacture: absolutely pure."—The Analyst.
NO CHEMICALS USED
(As in the so-called pure Foreign Cocoas).

some manufacturers mixed this waste material with the nibs to bulk out the end product. This fraud was particularly common in Ireland where it was legal to import the husks independent of the beans, incurring a much lower duty than whole nibs. 'How scurvily the people of Ireland are treated by their own grocers! Upwards of 60,000 lbs of worthless cocoa-husks served out to them along with only 4,000 lbs of cocoa-beans!' exclaimed chemist Alexander Ure (1778–1857). Even after the introduction of the Sale of Food and Drugs Act 1875 (which repealed the earlier Food Adulteration Acts of 1860 and 1872), designed to clarify what was deemed to be an adulterant, the argument rumbled on into the next century. In a 1910 court case concerning the sale of cocoa that was found to contain 65 per cent powdered cocoa husks, part of the defence was that the husk contained a greater quantity of theobromine than the nib and therefore provided superior health benefits to the consumer. As no starch had been added to this cocoa, it did not infringe the Act. The defence also argued that in the absence of any agreed standard for cocoa it was perfectly acceptable to use the whole bean. The prosecutor contested that the powdered shells must have been incorporated after processing by the grocer, William Davies, so the product was clearly adulterated. In the end, the magistrate, Mr Fordham, concluded that if cocoa contained more than 7 per cent of husk the consumer should be made aware that they were purchasing a lower grade of cocoa. As Mr Davies had not made this clear on the cocoa he had sold, he was fined 40s plus 5 guineas costs.

In present-day mass-chocolate production some additional ingredients beyond cocoa mass, cocoa butter, sugar and milk (in milk chocolate) are tolerated. The accepted standard by most consumers for quality dark chocolate is a minimum of 70 per cent cocoa solids. Fine milk chocolate should contain at least 30 per cent cocoa solids. The issue of emulsification has been solved with the inclusion of lecithin from sunflower seeds or soybeans. Lecithin makes the chocolate more manageable, particularly when moulding into bars or enrobing

A surprising augmentation was made by German chocolatier Hildebrand, which began adding methamphetamine to their chocolate assortments in the 1930s. At the time methamphetamine, sold under the brand name Pervitin, was hailed as something of a wonder drug. It had the ability to energise, improve confidence and even increase libido in women. The methamphetamine-laden confectionery was marketed with the tagline 'Hildebrand chocolates are always a delight!' and was aimed at the German housewife. Between three and nine of these sweets would ensure that the housework was done in a trice and keep the lady of the house trim to boot, as methamphetamine also doubled as an appetite suppressant. Within a few years German scientists began to note the side effects of long-term methamphetamine use, such as lethargy, cognitive disturbance and depression. As a result, the Reich Health Office suspended the manufacture of these high-dosage chocolates, although Pervitin in tablet form remained in circulation.

confectionery. Stubbe's favourite spice, vanilla, is often included too, although the synthetic stuff, vanillin, is frowned upon by purists. That said, many craft chocolate makers argue that vanilla is only added to mask poor-quality beans, so the jury is still out on this additive.

Today, serious health concerns relating to chocolate are more likely to be associated with chemical pollution or pathogens. In June 2006 Cadbury were forced to recall three million chocolate bars over fears they had been contaminated with salmonella. The firm faced criticism for covering up the incident, which had occurred in the January of that year. Cadbury responded that the level of contamination was low, so there was no risk to human health. The recall had been a precautionary measure, although they failed to explain why it took them six months to implement. Perhaps even more disturbing than food poisoning is the potential risk from radioactive contamination. Following the Japanese nuclear disaster at Fukushima in 2011, there were fears that radiation-polluted foods, like chocolate bars, would find their way into British supermarkets after being falsely labelled by fraudsters as originating in Tokyo. This deception was uncovered by Taiwanese investigators in 2015, who identified 100 radioactive food products from Fukushima in their stores. However, radiation and food-poisoning scares aside, today's consumer is more likely to be concerned about the ethical nature of the chocolate they consume.

ETHICAL CHOCOLATE

Tell Mr Cadbury from me that cocoa is blood.

William E. Fay, missionary of the American Board of
Commissioners for Foreign Missions, Angola, 1906.

AT THE TURN OF the twentieth century, rumours of slavery
in the cacao-producing islands of São Tomé and Príncipe
began to filter back to George Cadbury. These Portuguese
colonies were situated off the west coast of Africa, and
in 1900 Cadbury had sourced 45 per cent of their cacao
from these islands. As Quakers, the Cadbury family had
actively campaigned against slavery so the thought that
their company could be inadvertently profiting from slave
labour was intolerable to George and his nephew William
(1867–1957), who by this date headed up the organisation.

Slavery had been an unpalatable feature of cacao
production for centuries. By the end of the seventeenth
century only 10 per cent of the original indigenous
population of the Americas remained. Mistreatment at the
hands of the Spanish invaders, and European diseases,

against which the Indians had no protection, decimated their numbers. This left the cacao plantation owners with a shortage of labour. The answer came in the guise of Africans who were transported against their will from the coast of West Africa to the Americas.

Slavery had officially been abolished by the governments of Britain, in 1833, and Portugal, in 1869. The rulings extended to all their colonies but suffered something of a liberal interpretation. The Portuguese realised that their colonies in São Tomé and Príncipe provided ideal growing conditions for cacao and duly transplanted cuttings from South America to the islands in 1824. By the end of the nineteenth century, it was one of the islands' principal exports, and cacao production had spread to other colonies in West Africa such as the Gold Coast (modern-day Ghana). However, the available workforce on São Tomé and Príncipe was insufficient for the Portuguese colonists' needs so more labourers were sourced from Angola. The Portuguese government claimed these *serviçais* (meaning servants) were willing labourers who signed five-year contracts to work in the islands' cacao plantations known as *roças*. This implied that a worker could choose to return to their homeland once the contract expired. In reality, the contracts automatically renewed. Although the serviçais were paid, the money could only be spent in the roça's store, ensuring it made its way back into the plantation owners' pockets. The serviçais were known to sing a song that included the line 'In São Tomé there's a door for going in, but none for going out.'

Campaigning journalist Henry Woodd Nevinson (1856–1941) had decided to undertake his own investigations into the cocoa slave trade in West Africa, eventually leading to the publication of his book *A Modern Slavery* (1906). Beginning his journey in Angola, Nevinson found covert human trafficking alive and well. 'Call slaves by another name, legalise their position by a few printed papers, and the traffic becomes a commercial enterprise deserving of every encouragement,' he opined. The serviçais were too terrified of the traffickers to object to their sale and considered a placement in São Tomé to be the equivalent of a life sentence in hell. On his journey into the Angolan interior he found physical evidence of the slave trade in the abandoned shackles and bones of those who had been unable to keep up with the march to the port cities like Benguela.

With agreement from the other major British chocolate producers, Fry and Rowntree, William Cadbury tasked fellow Quaker Joseph Burtt (1862–1939) with investigating the conditions of employment and labour on the chocolate islands. Burtt would spend five months on São Tomé visiting various roças, whose owners were only too happy to entertain him and show him around their properties. Burtt initially found the living and working conditions on many of the roças satisfactory, with most workers being treated reasonably, although it was clear that few, if any,

of the serviçais had the opportunity to leave their employ. He wrote often to Cadbury of the workers appearing fat and robust (possibly mistaking signs of malnutrition in children as healthy plumpness) but conceded that the death rate, attributed to anaemia and sleeping sickness, was worryingly high.

Burtt's travels would take him to Príncipe then on to Luanda and Angola. On the mainland he witnessed first-hand the evidence of slavery described by Nevinson.

It became blatantly obvious that the serviçais used to cultivate the cacao on São Tomé and Príncipe were forced to leave their homes in Angola against their will and enter a legal contract which was 'but a cloak to hide slavery'. Burtt outlined his findings in a report which he sent to Cadbury in 1907. The British Foreign Office asked for the report to be edited before it was officially published so as not to cause the Portuguese government, long-time allies of the British, too much offence. Cadbury recommended that British chocolate manufacturers should boycott cacao from São Tomé and in 1909 Fry and Rowntree joined him.

In the end it was not the ongoing debate about slavery on the chocolate islands that devastated the cacao industry on São Tomé. Over 27,000 tonnes of cacao had been exported from the island in 1917 but this dropped by 56 per cent the following year. There was a brief rally of supply levels in 1919, largely thanks to the planters flooding the market with stored cacao, but exports soon plummeted again. The reason for this decline was the cacao swollen shoot virus. Spread by insects, the virus initially significantly affects the yields of cacao pods, but within three to four years the trees usually die. Cacao importers looked to the European colonies in Africa, such as Ghana, Côte d'Ivoire and Nigeria, as an alternative source.

It would be comfortable to believe that the efforts of Cadbury, Burtt and Nevinson and numerous other campaigners in the early twentieth century had a lasting and positive effect on the controversy surrounding cacao production. Almost a century later media coverage of the child labour crisis in Côte d'Ivoire revealed little had changed. In September 2000 a British television documentary claimed that slavery existed on up to 90 per cent of Ivorian cocoa farms. At the beginning of the twenty-first century Côte d'Ivoire supplied more than 40 per cent of the cocoa consumed worldwide. The documentary claimed that hundreds of thousands of children from Mali, Togo and Burkina Faso were being forced to work long hours without any pay and were subject to beatings and other abuse. A survey conducted by the International Institute for Tropical Agriculture (IITA) in 2002 reduced the number of child slaves to tens of thousands and claimed that they worked voluntarily, being the offspring of the farmers' family. Precise figures seem semantic here. Any number of enforced labourers – whether it be one or a million – is too many. It leaves an unpleasant taste in the mouth to think that our most-loved chocolate bars could be a product of modern slavery.

The Cocoa Protocol, or Harkin–Engel Protocol, established in 2001 by US Senator Tom Harkin and Congressman Eliot Engel, pledged to reduce the worst forms of child labour by 70 per cent across the cocoa sectors of Ghana and Cote d'Ivoire by 2020. When 2020 arrived it was estimated that 60 per cent of the world's cocoa was produced by Côte d'Ivoire and Ghana, employing 1.56 million child labourers, most aged between twelve and sixteen, although some as young as five. Forty-three per cent of these youngsters are involved in hazardous activities, such as exposure to agro-chemicals, lifting heavy loads and using sharp tools like machetes, and have little opportunity for education. More than half are injured by their work. Poor farmers, who receive minimal return for their cacao, use child labour to decrease the cost of production. Côte d'Ivoire has the lowest daily income for cacao farmers of all the producing countries, sitting somewhere between $0.50 and $1.25 per day. Both countries have expressed their commitment to eliminating the worst forms of child labour but there is still a considerable mountain to climb to reach the Cocoa Protocol's goal.

If these facts and figures are designed to make the consumer feel guilty about buying sullied chocolate, then they are doing a grand job. Since the 1980s the concept of ethical consumption to instigate social change has been in the ascendancy. The ethical consumer wants to stick two proverbial fingers up to big business and provide unswerving support to the exploited underdog. Non-profit organisations such as the Rainforest Alliance and the Fairtrade Foundation have been helping people politely do just that for more than thirty years. Both run accreditation programmes to help farmers produce goods that meet specific economic, social and environmental sustainability criteria known as Voluntary Sustainability Standards (vss). Those that implement the standards can use the widely recognised logos on their products and differentiate themselves from other cacao farmers. The International Institute for Sustainable Development estimates that there are five to six million cacao farmers globally with 800,000 producing vss-compliant cocoa. Encouragingly up to 85 per cent of vss-compliant cocoa comes from Africa. However, as the authors of a report for UNICEF sadly stated in 2020, NPO certification is no guarantee that child labour was not used in the processing of the chocolate bar.

The good news is that there is an ever increasing number of bean-to-bar producers around the world. These manufacturers go to great lengths to source ethically sound beans from small cacao farmers, often visiting the plantations in person. This ensures the farmer gets a fair price for their crop, enabling them to pay their workers a wage. The bean-to-bar manufacturers often roast and process the beans themselves, which means they can produce high-quality chocolate on a small scale. Often, they will also tell you which country the beans were sourced from. The catch is that you can expect to pay well above what you would for a bog-standard, mass-produced chocolate bar. But surely it's worth the investment for the reassurance that it is not tainted by slavery?

INNOVATIVE CHOCOLATE

Simple businesses, that's what you need, if you wish to go for the world.

Forrest Mars (1904–1999)

THE CHOCOLATE business would not be the multibillion-dollar global industry it is today had its prize ingredient remained a beverage. Rapid industrialisation and chemical experimentation in the nineteenth century helped chocolate jump from the cup into our lunchboxes. The modern era of chocolate making began in 1828 when Coenraad van Houten (1801–1887) used a hydraulic press to extract a greater quantity of cocoa butter from the beans. The remaining cocoa mass was treated with alkaline salts (potassium or sodium carbonate) to remove the bitterness and improve its solubility, in a process known as 'Dutching'. This provides a chocolate liquor that can be further processed into cocoa powder or chocolate for confectionery. The darker, smoother Dutch cocoa quickly became the consumers' favourite. Given this defatting innovation it is easy to understand why the Lancet Sanitary Commission were reluctant to buy into the necessity for extra starch in cocoa to solve the solubility issue. In 1876 Swiss chocolate maker Rodolphe Lindt (1855–1909) developed a new machine with a conch-shell-shaped trough that repeatedly rolled and slapped the cacao paste against the sides of the trough for seventy-two hours. 'Conching', as the process became known, also allowed more cocoa butter to be introduced to the refined cacao paste, creating a lighter, finer, liquid chocolate ideal for moulding. Lindt appropriately dubbed this sleeker chocolate 'fondant' and it spelled the end for the slightly granular, hard chocolate bars of the past.

Up to the late nineteenth century, processed chocolate, whether it was for eating or drinking, was dark. Alsatian entrepreneur Daniel Peter (1836–1919), originally a candle maker, was married to the daughter of Swiss chocolatier François-Louis Cailler (1796–1852), Fanny-Louise. The idea for milk chocolate had been inspired by his friend and neighbour Henri Nestlé's (1814–1890) powdered milk baby formula that had come to the rescue of Peter's infant daughter when she refused to breastfeed. His initial trials with powdered milk proved unsuccessful so Peter switched to using condensed milk, eventually finding success with the world's first ready-made milk chocolate drink in 1875. Further experimentation led to the launch of a creamy, smooth, milk chocolate bar in 1886. Soon, chocolate makers on both sides of the Atlantic were adopting these

innovations to make more sophisticated chocolate for drinking and eating, with Cadbury launching their popular Dairy Milk bar in June 1905.

The innovations of van Houten, Lindt and Peter set the stage for new entrants into the chocolate market in the early twentieth century. On the other side of the Atlantic, Frank Mars (1883–1935) was becoming reacquainted with his son, Forrest, from whom he had become estranged

EAT MORE MILK

1½

GLASSES OF ENGLISH
FULL CREAM MILK
IN EVERY

½ lb

CADBURY'S
DAIRY CDM MILK
CHOCOLATE

after divorcing his mother. Frank, dubbed 'that miserable failure' by his ex-wife after a series of collapsed businesses, had finally found success with his Mars-O-Bar Company in the cities of Minneapolis and St Paul, selling gooey sweets made from caramel, nuts and chocolate. The hugely ambitious Forrest thought his father's business goals were too limited. Forrest wanted to build an empire selling their products all over the USA, if not the world. According to Forrest's version of events it was he who came up with the idea to turn a malted-milk chocolate drink into a candy bar. In 1924, the Mars-O-Bar Company launched the 'Milky Way', a malt-flavoured nougat made with cheap corn syrup and egg whites, topped with caramel and dipped in chocolate. It was economical to produce, tasted amazing and was an instant hit. In its launch year alone it grossed $800,000 sales. Within five years they had opened a factory in Chicago that was churning out twenty million Milky Way bars a year.

Although they looked alike Frank and Forrest had completely different personalities. After numerous business failures, Frank was cautious and steady. Forrest was a risk taker, boorish and constantly questioned his father's decisions. By 1932 Frank had become fed up with his son's abrasive, gung-ho management style and gave him his marching orders. Forrest left the USA with the foreign rights to produce the Milky Way and $50,000. After a brief stint on the Continent visiting European chocolate makers,

"When you crave   good candy"

he found his way to Slough, where he established a small production facility. His slightly sweeter version of the Milky Way, the Mars Bar, was launched in 1933. Forrest had even managed to persuade Cadbury to sell him the chocolate used to coat his bars. Given how successful Mars would become, this decision to provide support to the start-up company has perplexed members of the Cadbury family ever since, but then hindsight is a wonderful thing. The combination of nougat, caramel and familiar Cadbury chocolate meant the Mars Bar was an instant hit with the British public. By 1939 Mars Ltd was ranked as Britain's third largest chocolate confectioner.

Not long after the Mars Bar appeared in Europe, another newcomer entered the confectionery market. Nestlé added cocoa butter to their vitamin-enriched condensed milk, Nestrovit, designed as a health supplement for children, to create the first commercial white chocolate bar in 1936.

It was originally called Galak after the Dutch condensed milk company Nestlé owned, but was later rebranded as the Milky Bar. The debate over whether white chocolate is real chocolate has raged for almost a century now, but for the sake of argument I am including it here.

War was the recipe for success for another American chocolate maker, Milton Hershey (1857–1945). The Hershey Chocolate Company was established in 1900, and during the First World War Hershey provided the US army with chocolate bars. When the US went to war with Japan in 1941, Hershey's food technologists were tasked with creating a quarter-pound, high-energy bar, capable of withstanding temperatures of around 50°C and that tasted 'a little better than a boiled potato'. The result was the 600-calorie D-Ration bar made from chocolate, sugar, skimmed milk powder, cocoa fat, oat flour, artificial flavouring, and vitamin B1 to protect against beriberi (a disease leading to nerve inflammation and possibly heart failure caused by a deficiency of vitamin B1). Incredibly dense, the bar was designed as an emergency ration to be eaten slowly over a period of thirty minutes or dissolved in boiling water to create a beverage. It was not exactly popular with the troops and even the workers at the Hershey plant complained about handling the clay-like raw D-Ration mixture.

The US military chocolate bar was updated in the 1990s when Hershey created the Desert Bar to cope with

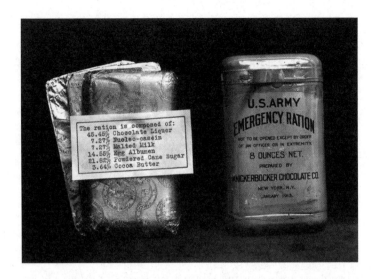

the climate in the Middle East during the Gulf War (1990–1991). This version was closer to a regular Hershey chocolate bar but could withstand temperatures of up to 60°C thanks in part to the addition of egg whites and other 'secret' ingredients. Instead of liquifying in extreme heat the Desert Bar turns soft and fudgy.

The German army had their own energy-boosting bar during the Second World War. Rather than their methamphetamine-spiked chocolates eaten by the nation's housewives, Hildebrand's Scho-Ka-Kola was laden with caffeine. Launched in 1935, it was originally aimed at athletes. The distinctive circular red tins held two discs, each divided into eight segments and containing the same amount of caffeine as a cup of coffee. Towards the end of the war this chocolate was issued to troops as a treat. Johann Voss, a Waffen-SS veteran, described the boxes as 'pure luxury' in his memoir *Black Edelweiss* (2002), adding that 'Such charity was an unmistakable sign that things were getting serious.' You can still buy Scho-Ka-Kola today.

Shortages of raw ingredients like cacao in the post-war communist People's Republic of Bulgaria forced food technologists to develop an alternative to traditional chocolate. Although the new confection was brown and labelled as chocolate, the cocoa content was minimal. The mixture was bulked out with hydrogenated fats, flavourings, sugar, fruit and soybean flour, and some varieties had a distinct petroleum taste. It was generally loathed by the Bulgarian population and was dubbed 'marzipan' despite having no resemblance to the almond paste confections available in Western Europe.

While the general populace in Bulgaria had to contend with fake chocolate, the politicians were eating quality chocolate made by the same factories with pure cacao. This was deemed a 'special purveyance', which covered the supply of the delicacies absent from the mass market to political elites like Georgi Dimitrov (1882–1949), the first Communist leader of Bulgaria. Polish chocolatiers presented Russian leader Joseph Stalin (1878–1953) with a cake adorned with a statue of himself made in chocolate, to celebrate the dictator's seventieth birthday. Artist Nikita Gusev has also recreated Stalin in chocolate form. His most

recent chocolate handiwork was a life-size sculpture of the Russian president Vladimir Putin for the St Petersburg Chocolate Festival in 2015, requiring more than 150 pounds of chocolate.

Chocolate has come a long way from the days of the Mesoamericans, when cacao was used as a currency as well as a ceremonial drink. In 2021, the chocolate confectionery market generated a revenue of approximately 0.99 trillion US dollars worldwide. Chocolate has even found its way into space. Russian cosmonaut Yuri Gagarin (1934–1968) ate chocolate sauce from a squeezable toothpaste-like tube on the first orbit of the Earth in 1961. Chocolate is requested by NASA astronauts on most flights into space, with M&Ms topping the bill. Forrest Mars would be chuffed to know that one of his products is conquering the final frontier.

HOW TO TASTE CHOCOLATE

*She felt in the pocket of her overalls and produced
a small slab of chocolate. She broke it in half and
gave one of the pieces to Winston. Even before he had
taken it he knew by the smell that it was very unusual
chocolate. It was dark and shiny, and was wrapped
in silver paper. Chocolate normally was dull-brown
crumbly stuff that tasted, as nearly as one could
describe it, like the smoke of a rubbish fire.*

George Orwell, *1984* (1949)

THERE IS CHOCOLATE and there is *chocolate*. Much of
the commercial mass-produced chocolate available in
our supermarkets is fairly banal from a connoisseur's
perspective, with artificial flavourings, milk powder and
preservatives drowning out cacao's true properties.

When the Europeans arrived in Central and South
America there were thought to be two varieties of
Theobroma cacao. *Criollo* is considered the most ancient
variety used by the Maya and Aztecs and the most revered

95

for its aroma and flavour. Unfortunately, it is quite finicky to grow, lower yielding and more susceptible to disease than the other variety, *forestero*. Forestero (meaning 'foreigner' in Spanish), originally from Ecuador, was more abundant although not as flavoursome as criollo. When disease attacked the criollo trees on the Caribbean island of Trinidad in the eighteenth century, a hybrid of criollo and forestero was created, and the *trinitario* variety was born. Modern science has identified thirteen distinct genetic varieties of cacao, making the term forestero redundant. These include criollo, *nacional* or *arriba* (from Ecuador and northern Peru) and *amelonado* (predominantly found in West Africa). The International Institute of Chocolate Tasting estimates there are hundreds of trinitario-style cacao hybrids now being grown across the world, each possessing its own characteristics.

Chocolate tasting is therefore a complex business. A high-quality chocolate will contain a myriad of flavours, including spicy, fruity, molasses and earthy notes. Levels of acidity and tannins will vary according to the type of cacao used and where it is grown, as well as the degree of roasting. If you thought the wine buffs had the monopoly on florid descriptions of the drinks they taste, think again. You can even attend courses now to become a fully fledged chocolate sommelier.

A similar approach to chocolate tasting is taken to sampling wine, taking into account its appearance and aroma before eating it. The following considerations should be made:

☞ How is the depth of colour? Very dark tones can indicate a high-roast and possibly defective cacao, which can result in a bitter-tasting chocolate. If the surface looks dusty, this indicates chocolate 'bloom'. This occurs when chocolate has been tempered incorrectly (see below) or has been stored at a high temperature.

☞ Does it have a pleasing snap when you break off a piece? If it does, it has been correctly tempered. This means the chocolate has been heated slowly then cooled so that the fat molecules crystallise evenly, resulting in a smooth, shiny finish when the chocolate sets.

☞ How does it smell? Approximately 80 to 90 per cent of our taste is based on the aroma of food. You may need to warm the chocolate up a little in your hands first to coax the scent out. Smell it several times before tasting it. If you are in any doubt, try eating a piece of chocolate while holding your nose – it will contain little or no flavour.

☞ Place the chocolate on your tongue then let it melt naturally. This will be torture for those who are used to munching their chocolate indiscriminately, but it really is the best way to taste chocolate. As it melts it will gradually unveil its flavours and allow you to assess the texture of the chocolate. Chocolate that contains a lot of cocoa butter, like milk chocolate, will melt more quickly than darker bars.

☞ A good chocolate will keep on giving in terms of flavour even after you have swallowed it, and is said to possess good length. Sourness or metallic tastes can be a sign that the roasting was poorly executed or the cacao is inferior.

COOKING CHOCOLATE

CHOCOLATE & HAZELNUT CAKE
Makes 10–12 slices

Chocolate and hazelnut spread beloved by children across Europe inadvertently came about as a result of ingredient shortages in Italy caused by the Second World War. It's a cracking combo and it's easy to see why it remains popular.

50g chopped roasted hazelnuts or ground almonds
100g plain flour
50g cocoa powder
2 tsp baking powder
225g golden caster sugar
225g unsalted butter, softened,
plus extra for greasing

4 large eggs
1 tsp vanilla extract
200g chocolate and hazelnut spread
75g dark chocolate
75g milk chocolate
150ml double cream
1½ tbsp amaretto (optional)

1. Grease and line the bases of two 20cm (8in) sandwich tins. Preheat the oven to 180°C.
2. Use a food processor to finely grind the hazelnuts to a coarse powder (if using hazelnuts rather than ground almonds).
3. Sift the flour, cocoa powder and baking powder into a bowl. Stir in the ground hazelnuts or ground almonds.
4. In a separate bowl, cream the sugar and butter together until light and fluffy, using an electric whisk or a wooden spoon.
5. Beat in one of the eggs followed by about a quarter of the flour mixture, mixing thoroughly to combine. Repeat with the remaining eggs and flour, mixing between each addition. Finally, stir in the vanilla extract.
6. Divide the mixture between the two tins, spreading evenly. Bake for 15–20 minutes until well risen and springy (a skewer should come out clean

when inserted into the centre of the sponges). Allow to cool in the tins before turning out onto a wire rack.

7. When the sponges are cool, sandwich together with the chocolate and hazelnut spread.

8. To make the icing, place the dark and milk chocolate and the cream in a heatproof bowl. Suspend the bowl over a pan of barely simmering water, ensuring the bottom of the bowl doesn't touch the water. Stir occasionally until the chocolate has melted, then add the amaretto (if using). Allow the ganache to cool and thicken to a spreadable consistency.

9. Use a palette knife to coat the sides and top of the cake with the icing, then place in the fridge to firm up before serving.

'OLD WORLD' SPICED HOT CHOCOLATE
Serves 2-3

This is how I imagine early chocolate drinks would have tasted. If you prefer a plainer version by all means omit the dried spices. It is a very rich drink so a little goes a long way.

4–5cm (1½–2in) piece cinnamon stick
½ tsp black peppercorns

¼ tsp aniseeds
¼ whole nutmeg, grated
80g dark chocolate, chopped into small pieces
2 tbsp dark brown sugar
1 tsp vanilla extract
500ml whole milk or dairy-free milk
Grated nutmeg or ground cinnamon,
to serve (optional)

1. Using a pestle and mortar or the end of a rolling pin, coarsely crush the cinnamon, peppercorns and aniseeds. Stir in the grated nutmeg.
2. Place the chocolate, dark brown sugar and vanilla in a mixing bowl.
3. Pour the milk into a saucepan, then add the crushed spices. Slowly bring the milk up to boiling point, then gradually strain over the chocolate and sugar in the bowl, stirring after each addition until the chocolate has melted.
4. Rinse the saucepan to ensure there are no spices left in it. Pour the chocolate mixture into the pan and reheat gently until hot but not boiling. Pour into cups and serve immediately. Dust with a light grating of nutmeg or ground cinnamon if desired.

GLOSSARY OF TERMS

ACHIOTE Also known as annatto, this is a natural orange-red food colourant from the *Bixa orellana* shrub, native to Central America.

AMBERGRIS A solid, grey substance vomited up by sperm whales. It is highly prized by the perfume industry but was also used in the past as a spice in culinary recipes.

BLOOM This term is applied to the dusty, chalky appearance on the surface of chocolate. The condition occurs when chocolate has been stored at too high a temperature, causing the cocoa butter to melt, or when moisture has come into contact with the surface of the chocolate.

COCOA BUTTER Depending on the variety, cacao beans have a fat content of between 52 and 57 per cent. This is referred to as cocoa butter. Although it is used to produce modern chocolate bars, much of it is deodorised and used in the cosmetics industry.

COCOA MASS The residue left after the cocoa butter has been removed (around 48–43 per cent of the original bean). This is the basis of cocoa powder.

Cocoa Solids The term for the combination of cocoa butter and cocoa mass found in a chocolate bar. In fine dark chocolate this will be over 60 per cent and in milk it will be over 30 per cent.

Conching A process for refining cacao that takes its name from the shell-like shape of a machine invented by Rodolphe Lindt. The cacao paste is repeatedly rolled for up to seventy-two hours until a smooth liquor is produced. The resulting chocolate is silky, as the process allows for the introduction of extra cocoa butter.

Dutching Invented by Coenraad van Houten, this process removes much of the fat from the cacao. The remaining cacao mass is combined with alkaline salts to improve its solubility.

Enrobing A mechanical process for coating chocolate sweets.

Lecithin A food additive made from fatty acids typically found in egg yolks, sunflower seeds or soybeans. It is commonly added to mass-produced chocolate to improve its viscosity.

Tempering This is a critical process in the production of chocolate. The temperature of the liquid chocolate is raised and then lowered to avoid the formation of crystals in the solid chocolate, which can appear mottled and discoloured in a condition known as 'bloom'.

Winnowing A process that removes the husk of the beans to allow them to be processed into cocoa nibs.

FURTHER READING

Deborah Cadbury, *Chocolate Wars: From Cadbury to Kraft: 200 Years of Sweet Success and Bitter Rivalry* (Harper Press, 2010)

Sophie D. Coe and Michael D. Coe, *The True History of Chocolate* (Thames & Hudson, 2019)

Catherine Higgs, *Chocolate Islands: Cocoa, Slavery, and Colonial Africa* (Ohio University Press, 2012)

Emma Kay, *A Dark History of Chocolate* (Pen & Sword, 2021)

Sue Quinn, *Cocoa: An Exploration of Chocolate, with Recipes* (Hardie Grant, 2019)

Emma Robertson, *Chocolate, Women and Empire: A Social and Cultural History* (Manchester University Press, 2009)

Henry Stubbe, *The Indian Nectar, or, A Discourse Concerning Chocolata* (printed by J. C. for Andrew Crook, London, 1662)

LIST OF ILLUSTRATIONS

All images from the collections of the British Library unless otherwise stated.

Also available in this series

THE PHILOSOPHY OF
COCKTAILS
JANE PEYTON
BRITISH LIBRARY

THE PHILOSOPHY OF
WHISKY
BILLY ABBOTT

THE PHILOSOPHY OF
CURRY
SEJAL SUKHADWALA
BRITISH LIBRARY

THE PHILOSOPHY OF
TEA
TONY GEBELY

THE PHILOSOPHY OF
WINE
RUTH BALL

THE PHILOSOPHY OF
GIN
JANE PEYTON

THE PHILOSOPHY OF
BEER
JANE PEYTON

THE PHILOSOPHY OF
CHEESE
PATRICK McGUIGAN

THE PHILOSOPHY OF
COFFEE
BRIAN WILLIAMS
BRITISH LIBRARY